All About Birds

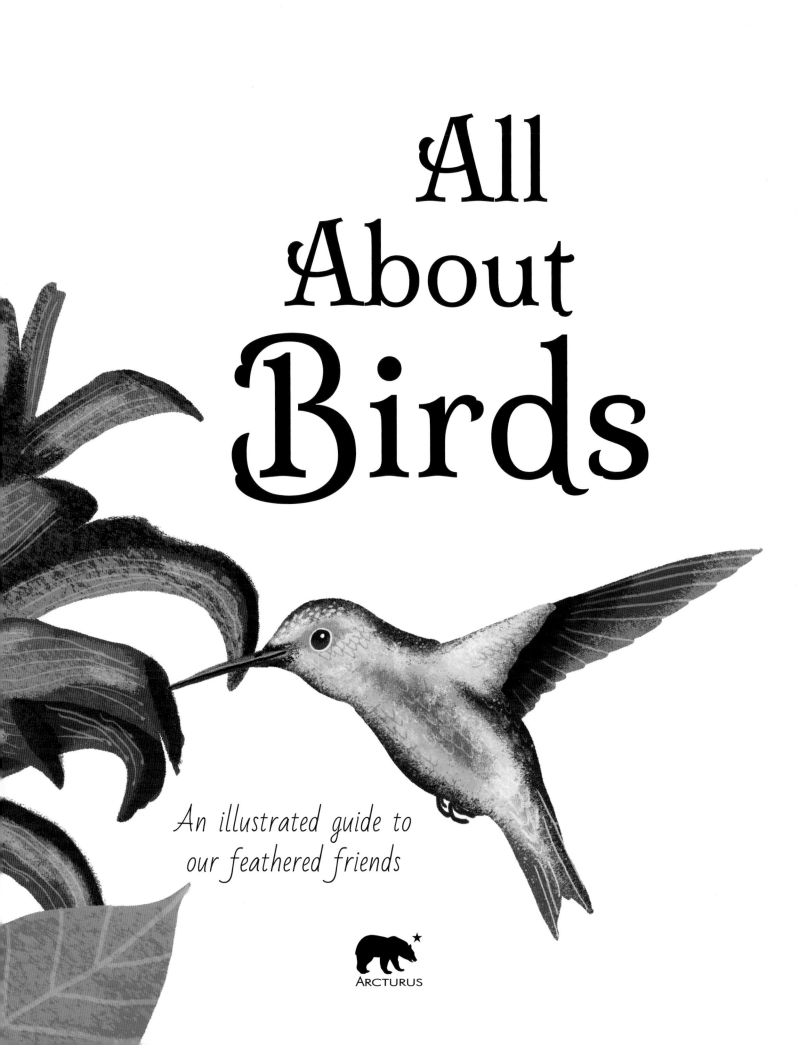

An illustrated guide to our feathered friends

ARCTURUS

ARCTURUS

This edition published in 2022 by Arcturus Publishing Limited
26/27 Bickels Yard, 151–153 Bermondsey Street,
London SE1 3HA

Author: Polly Cheeseman
Illustrator: Iris Deppe
Designer: Stefan Holliland
Editor: Violet Peto
Consultant: Anne Rooney
Managing Editor: Joe Harris

ISBN: 978-1-3988-1992-4
CH010041NT
Supplier 29, Date 0622, PI 00002184

Printed in China

Contents

Beautiful Birds

From the frozen ice sheets of Antarctica, to the dry deserts of Africa, birds live all over the world. They come in lots of different shapes and sizes, but all birds have some things in common.

Flight feathers

Birds are the only animals that have feathers. Feathers keep birds warm, dry, and help them fly. Birds keep their feathers clean with their beaks.

Eurasian jay

All birds hatch from eggs. The chicks grow inside the eggs. Bird parents sit on their eggs to keep them warm until they are ready to hatch.

Instead of teeth, birds have beaks. A bird's beak is perfectly shaped for the type of food it eats. This jay uses its strong bill to crack open acorns.

All birds have wings, but not all birds can fly. Flying birds have strong chest muscles, which help them beat their wings.

Expert Hunters

The group of birds that hunt for their food and attack with their claws are called **birds of prey**. Among the largest and most powerful birds of prey are eagles.

Bald eagle

Eagles have amazing eyesight that is more than twice as sharp as a human's. Eagles can spot their **prey** from high up in the sky.

The Andean condor is the largest and heaviest bird of prey. It has a wingspan of 3 m (10 ft). These birds feed on the bodies of dead animals, such as deer and cows.

Its huge wings let the eagle glide easily through the air. It soars high up to get a good view of animals below, then swoops down to attack.

Eagles have very strong, sharp claws called **talons**. Bald eagles use their talons to catch fish, grasping them tightly until they reach their nests.

Birds of prey have powerful beaks that are hooked and very sharp.

The peregrine falcon is the world's fastest-flying bird. When it spots prey, it pulls in its wings and dives down to attack at speeds of more than 250 kph (155 mph).

Nest Building

Most birds build nests. These are safe places, where eggs and chicks can be protected from **predators**. Nests can be made from lots of different materials, including twigs, moss, mud, and spiderwebs.

Tailorbirds live in Asia. They get their name from the way they build their nests. They "sew" leaves using their beaks, like a tailor sews cloth.

The male tailorbird gathers the materials and keeps watch.

Ovenbirds collect mud and place it on a tree branch. Bit by bit, more mud is added to form a rounded shape. The mud nest bakes hard in the sun.

To make their nests, woodpeckers carve a hole in a tree using their strong beaks. When the hole is ready, they lay their eggs inside.

First, a female tailorbird finds a strong leaf, which is still attached to the tree. She makes tiny holes along the leaf using her needle-sharp beak.

The female uses tiny strands of plants and spiderwebs to stitch the leaf into a cup shape.

Spiderweb thread

The male tailorbird helps fill the leaf with soft pieces of plants, animal fur, and feathers. The nest is made so carefully that the leaf stays green and alive!

Woodpecker

Being waterbirds, swans need to build their large nests close to the water's edge. The nest is a huge mound of grasses, rushes, and other plants.

9

Bringing up Blue Tits

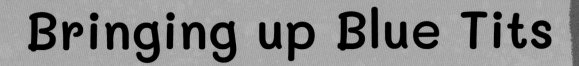

Every spring, adult blue tits prepare to raise a family. They look for holes in trees, walls, or use human-made birdhouses. Discover how these pretty birds hatch and grow during their first weeks of life.

The female makes a cup-shaped nest in a nesting hole using moss, grass, and leaves. She lines it with soft feathers and animal hair.

The blue tit lays one egg a day. She lays around 10 eggs altogether. While she sits on the eggs to keep them warm, her partner brings her food.

After two weeks, the eggs are ready to hatch. Blue tit chicks are blind, featherless, and helpless when they hatch. The mother sits on them to keep them warm.

Both parents feed the chicks with hundreds of fresh caterpillars throughout the day. The chicks' mouths are bright yellow— easy for the parents to see.

The chicks grow quickly. After just a few weeks, they can begin flying. The chick is now called a **fledgling**. Chicks leave the nest a few weeks later.

City Birds

Many different birds have adapted to life in towns and cities. Birds make their calls louder to be heard over the traffic noise. They also depend on people for some of their food.

Blue jay

Pretty house finches like to visit people's backyards. As well as gobbling up insects, finches love to eat sunflower seeds from bird feeders.

American robin

European starling

American crows are not fussy about their food—they eat pretty much anything they can find! They gather in large groups to **roost** at night.

House sparrows hop around busy areas, looking for crumbs to peck. Some sparrows are so friendly, they will even eat from your hand!

Northern cardinal

Pigeons are a common sight on city streets. They can be seen perching on buildings and under bridges. They often eat food that people have dropped.

Make a Bird Feeder

Want to attract birdlife to your backyard? Get busy in the kitchen and make this tasty treat. Then sit back and wait for your feathered friends!

Ask a grown-up to help you make a hole through the middle of an apple using a skewer or apple corer.

Push some string through the hole in the apple. Tie the string around a thin stick or chopstick, so that the apple sits on top.

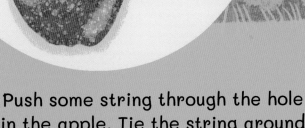

Carefully push seeds into the apple skin, until the apple is covered. Sunflower seeds work well for this—and birds love them!

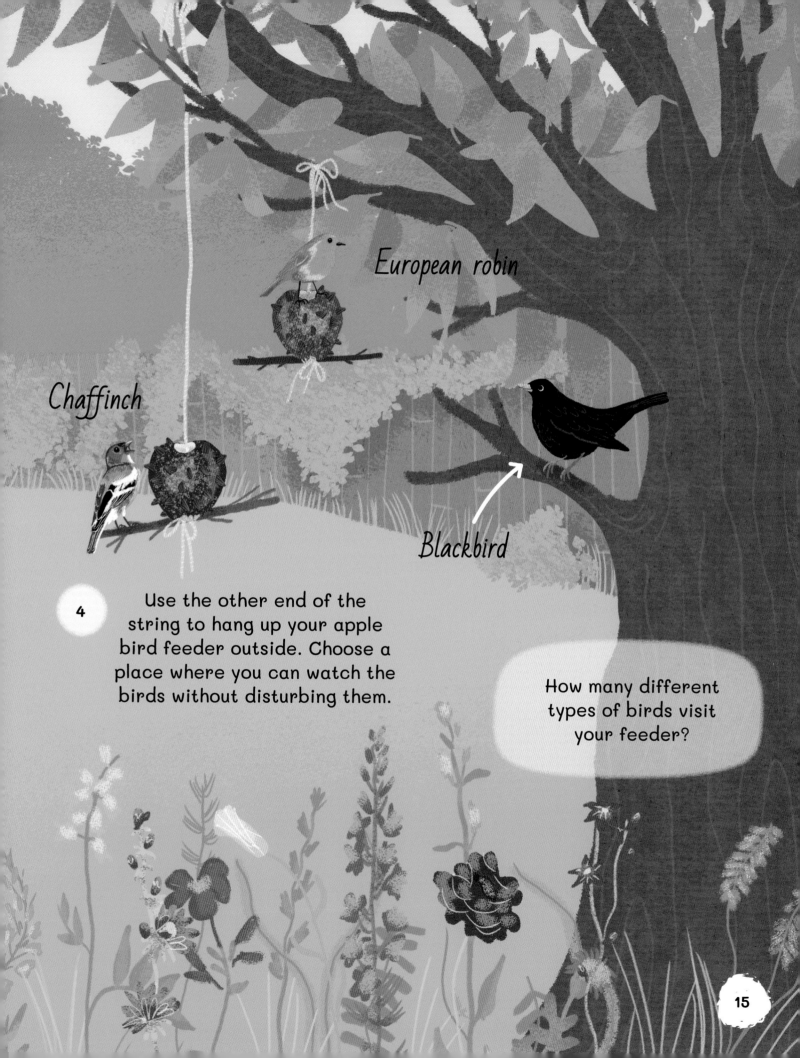

European robin

Chaffinch

Blackbird

4 Use the other end of the string to hang up your apple bird feeder outside. Choose a place where you can watch the birds without disturbing them.

How many different types of birds visit your feeder?

Brilliant Beaks

The shape of a bird's beak, or bill, helps it eat the type of food it likes. Toucans are well known for their huge beaks, which they use to eat fruit.

Toucans live in **rain forest** trees in South America. They use their long bills to reach fruits growing high up in the forest **canopy**.

Toco toucan

The northern shoveler is a "dabbling" duck, which means that it feeds at the water's surface. Its wide, flat bill acts like a sieve, filtering insects and plants to eat.

Finches, such as the Atlantic canary, have cone-shaped beaks. This shape makes the beak powerful enough to crack open the hard seeds that finches love.

The toucan's bill is very long compared to its body. The bill is around one-third of the bird's total body length!

The edges of the toucan's beak are jagged, or "serrated." This means that it can get a firm grip on its meal.

The beak is hollow, which makes it lightweight despite its size. The toucan's tongue is long and shaped a little bit like a feather.

Atlantic canary

The long, curved bill of the curlew is perfect for digging up food from mud. This wading bird uses its beak like tweezers to pluck out tiny creatures.

Emperor Penguin

The emperor penguin cannot fly, but it is an expert swimmer! These large birds are perfectly adapted to life in Antarctica—the coldest place on Earth.

Emperor penguins have a thick layer of fat under their skin. This keeps them warm. Their feathers are packed tightly together to keep out the freezing wind.

Emperor penguin chicks are covered with fluffy feathers. The parents keep their chick snug by balancing it on their feet, away from the icy ground.

Chick

Emperor penguins live in large groups called colonies. The **colony** huddles together for warmth. Each penguin takes its turn standing on the outside, where it's coldest.

Penguins use their small wings as flippers to power through the water. They can dive for nearly half an hour, hunting fish and other sea creatures.

Down by the River

Many different birds make their homes in and around rivers and streams. Waterbirds spend much of their time swimming and feeding. Other birds watch for fish from the riverbank.

Mallard

Common kingfisher

Ducks, such as mallards, have webbed feet, which are perfect for paddling through the water. They dip their heads under the surface to feed on water plants.

The bright and beautiful kingfisher will wait patiently on a branch for its next meal to swim by. It nests in a burrow on the riverbank.

20

Herons keep perfectly still for a long time. When they spot a tasty-looking fish, they plunge their long, stabbing beaks into the water.

Swans are large waterbirds that weigh around the same a as 7-year-old child. They use their long necks to reach for plants under the water.

Fantastic Fliers

Being able to fly allows birds to escape enemies, find food, or travel to warmer places. Different birds fly in different ways, depending on the size and shape of their wings.

Pigeons and doves fly by flapping their pointed wings continuously, so they have strong chest muscles to power them. They can fly at speeds of 80 kph (50 mph).

The tail helps the bird steer. It is also used for balance when the bird perches on a branch or walks on the ground.

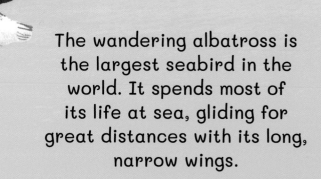

The wandering albatross is the largest seabird in the world. It spends most of its life at sea, gliding for great distances with its long, narrow wings.

Eurasian collared dove

The largest and strongest feathers are the flight feathers. The different parts of each feather link together to make a flat surface.

A bird's skeleton needs to be tough, but lightweight, in order to fly. Flying birds have hollow bones with special struts inside to make them superstrong.

Flight feathers

Many small birds, such as the chickadee, have rounded wings. Chickadees fly by flapping their wings quickly, then gliding in order to save energy.

Fabulous Flamingos

With their huge beaks, long legs, and bright pink feathers, flamingos are amazing-looking birds. They live in large colonies on the edges of lakes, or near shallow areas of water.

Flamingos are very noisy. Although there can be thousands of flamingos in a **colony**, a parent can find its chick by listening for its own special call.

Flamingos eat **plankton**, which is made up of tiny plants and animals. The plankton contains chemicals that turn flamingo feathers pink or red.

Flamingos are often seen standing on one leg, but it isn't known why. When looking for a **mate**, a group of flamingos will perform a kind of dance together!

When a flamingo feeds, it turns its head upside down and puts its beak under the water. The beak has bristles inside, which trap the plankton.

Nighttime Birds

Just like us, most birds are active during the day.

But when the sun goes down, some birds are getting ready for the night ahead. Owls are the best-known **nocturnal** birds.

Owls have super senses. Their large eyes see extremely well in dim light. They also have excellent hearing and can hear tiny creatures from far away.

Nightjars are nocturnal birds with mottled, brown feathers. As they fly, they open their beaks wide to catch nighttime insects, such as moths.

Unlike other birds, owls have large, forward-facing eyes. This means it can spot movement and judge distance from high above its **prey**.

The edges of an owl's flight feathers are fringed and soft. This allows the owl to fly very quietly, so its prey doesn't hear it coming.

The great horned owl is the largest owl in North America. It is a fierce **predator** and sometimes hunts other owls.

The kiwi is a fluffy-looking **flightless bird** from New Zealand. It walks about at night, sniffing out worms, insects, and fallen fruit to eat.

During the day, the black-crowned night heron **roosts** in trees close to wetlands. At sunset, it comes out to feed on fish and other creatures.

Along the Coast

Lots of birds can be seen by the seashore, because there is plenty of food here. Some birds catch fish at sea, while others wait on the beach to see what's been washed up.

Cormorants nest in cliffs along the coastline. They are excellent swimmers and will dive under the water to catch fish with their hooked beaks.

Fluttering among the rocks, the turnstone flips stones looking for food underneath. It can turn over rocks the same size as its body!

Gulls are a common sight and sound on the coast. Herring gulls don't just eat herrings. They will eat almost anything they can find!

Oystercatchers are wading birds. They walk along the shoreline, using their long beaks to crack open shellfish, such as cockles and mussels.

Ringed plover

Incredible Divers

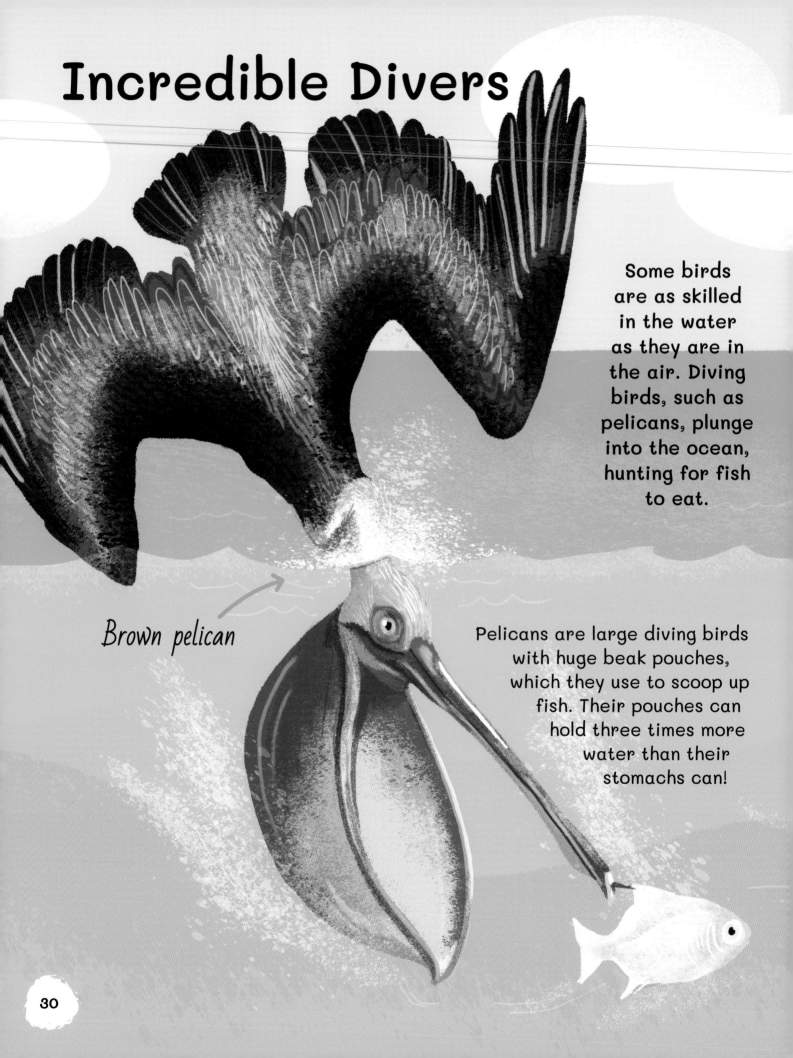

Some birds are as skilled in the water as they are in the air. Diving birds, such as pelicans, plunge into the ocean, hunting for fish to eat.

Brown pelican

Pelicans are large diving birds with huge beak pouches, which they use to scoop up fish. Their pouches can hold three times more water than their stomachs can!

The brown pelican hunts by flying over the surface of the ocean and diving in head first. It takes in large gulps of water and fish.

The pelican pushes the water out of its bill with its throat muscles. Then, it swallows the fish left inside its beak.

The Atlantic puffin dives from the water's surface, using its wings like flippers. Its bright bill has jagged edges, allowing it to hold up to 60 small fish at once!

As well as being expert divers, pelicans can glide long distances using their extremely large wings. Their wingspan is greater than the height of a man.

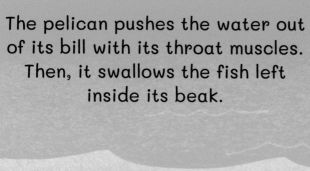

Pretty Parrots

With their bright feathers and noisy squawks, parrots are very clever and friendly birds. Macaws are a type of parrot that lives in warm, **tropical rain forests** in South America.

Blue and gold macaw

Macaws are large, fast-flying parrots with long tails. They live high up in tall rain forest trees. Macaws stay with the same partner for life.

The cockatoo uses its striking head **crest** to let others know how it's feeling. It raises its crest if it is excited or surprised.

Cockatiels are small and slim members of the cockatoo family. They live in Australia and make their nests in tree holes.

Scarlet macaw

There are lots of different kinds of macaws, each with their own markings. The scarlet macaw has a red head and body, and bright blue and yellow wings.

Macaws eat fruit, nuts, and seeds. Their powerful bills crack open seeds and rip fruit apart. Their tongues contain a bone, helping them open nuts.

Macaws often feed together in large, noisy groups. Sometimes, they gather on clay cliffs to nibble and lick the mineral-rich clay.

Clay cliff

Lovebirds are small parrots that live in dry areas of Africa. They are called lovebirds because of the close bond a pair of these birds makes.

Patterns in the Sky

As the sun goes down, thousands of starlings take to the skies and perform amazing flying displays. They fly together in a huge, swooping, moving shape called a **murmuration**.

At first glance, European starlings look like somewhat plain birds. Close up, you'll see their beautiful, glossy feathers with a green and purple sheen.

Winter is a good time to see a starling murmuration. This is when starling **flocks** are at their largest and their displays are the most spectacular.

Birds gather in large flocks for safety. It is harder for **predators**, such as peregrine falcons, to pick out one starling in a huge group.

Starlings murmurate just before they **roost** for the night. They roost close together in sheltered places, such as under buildings and cliffs, keeping each other warm.

Running Free

Not all birds can fly. To escape danger, some flightless birds have become super-speedy sprinters.

Male ostrich

Female ostrich

The largest and fastest of all flightless birds is the ostrich, which lives on grasslands in Africa.

The ostrich is the world's largest bird. It can grow much taller than a man and weigh twice as much. Its huge eyes are bigger than its brain!

Chicks

Emus are Australia's largest bird. Like their ostrich cousins, they can live in groups. They have long, shaggy tail feathers, which they shake to warn off predators.

Long, strong legs enable the ostrich to run at speeds of 70 kph (43 mph) to escape predators. Its kick is powerful enough to kill a lion.

The ostrich has long, fluffy wing feathers that help it change direction when running fast. An ostrich parent uses its wings to shade its chicks from the sun.

Given its size, it's not surprising that the ostrich lays the world's largest egg. Each egg weighs 30 times more than a chicken egg!

The cassowary sports a bright blue face and neck, and a horny head **crest**. It also has extremely long, knife-like claws, which it uses to defend itself.

Hummingbirds

Beating their wings faster than you can see, these tiny birds have incredible flying skills. Hummingbirds are only found in North and South America, and most types live in **tropical** forests.

Hummingbirds have long, slim bills and even longer tongues. They hover by flowers, pushing their beaks deep inside to drink the **nectar**. They also eat insects.

With their bright, shimmering feathers, hummingbirds look like jewels in the sky. Emerald hummingbirds are named for their sparkling green feathers.

Hummingbird feathers make reflect light, creating a shiny, rainbow effect called "iridescence." Males show off their glittering feathers to attract a **mate**.

Western emerald hummingbird

Hummingbirds can beat their wings 80 times a second, which makes a humming sound. These birds can hover, fly backward, and even fly upside down!

There are around 300 different kinds of hummingbird. At just 5 cm (2 in) long, the bee hummingbird is the smallest bird in the world.

Make a Birdbath

Birds need water to drink and to bathe in. It's important for birds to keep their feathers clean. Taking a dip loosens dirt and makes their feathers easier to look after.

Find a good spot to build your birdbath. An open area is best, so birds have a good view all around them.

Stack up some bricks, or upturned flowerpots, so that your birdbath is off the ground. Make sure you have a stable base.

Bricks

Stones

Place a large shallow dish or circular plant tray on top of the base. Make sure it is heavy enough to be stable. If there is any danger of your birdbath being blown over, ask an adult to strengthen it with superglue.

Flowerpots

Why not decorate your birdbath?

Fill your birdbath with water. Add stones and gravel to make sure it's not too slippery for your feathered friends!

Flying South

Every year, many birds make a very long journey. Birds fly great distances from their summer homes to where they spend the winter. The journey they make is called a **migration**.

Snow geese spend the summer nesting in the Arctic tundra. When it gets colder, the geese fly 1,250 km (2,000 mi) to the Western United States and Mexico.

The geese fly in a V-shape. Each goose follows the bird in front, so they all fly in the same direction. They are careful not to fly into each other.

Snow geese like company when they travel. There can be tens of thousands of snow geese in a **flock**. They can be very noisy!

Along the way, the geese make stops to rest and feed. Some birds will act as lookouts for the flock, watching for predators, such as eagles.

Birds of Paradise

Some creatures go to great lengths in order to find a **mate**. The birds of paradise are a group of birds with beautiful feathers, unusual calls, and very interesting dance moves!

Birds of paradise live in **tropical rain forests** on islands in the Pacific Ocean. There are many kinds, each with their own amazing feathers and displays.

Female birds of paradise are much plainer than the males. Females make sure that they choose the male with the most beautiful feathers.

Female

Males spend a lot of time preparing their display areas. They clear away sticks and prune leaves, so that females get a clear view of them.

The Goldie's bird of paradise puffs up long, fluffy feathers on his back and flaps his wings. He hops about, calling loudly to attract a female.

Goldie's bird of paradise

When he displays, the male superb bird of paradise flicks up his feathers into a cloak-like fan. Bright blue chest and head feathers make him look like a strange smiley face!

From this ...

... to this!

Birds Under Threat

Sadly, some birds are in danger. Forest homes are being cut down. Beautiful birds are captured for people to keep as pets. Others are harmed by chemicals.

California condors are **birds of prey** with wingspans of around 3 m (10 ft). Instead of hunting **prey**, they eat animals that are already dead.

The African grey, or African gray, is a beautiful parrot with an amazing ability to copy human voices. Many are stolen from their forest homes to become pets.

The kakapo is a large flightless parrot from New Zealand. It has been hunted by animals, such as cats and rats, which were introduced by people.

Condors have been killed by chemicals that have polluted their **habitat**. Others die because they eat animals that contain harmful substances.

In 1987, there were just 27 California condors left. To keep them from dying out, the last condors were captured and protected in zoos.

A few years later, some California condors were released back into the wild. There are now thought to be around 300 of these magnificent birds.

Kakapo

Kirtland's warblers were once in danger of dying out. Thankfully, their pine forest homes in North America have been protected. Now they are no longer **endangered**!

GLOSSARY

Birds of prey A group of birds that hunt animals using their claws.

Canopy The top layer of trees in a forest.

Colony A group of animals that live together.

Crest A natural growth on the head of an animal.

Endangered A living thing that is in danger of dying out.

Fledgling A young bird that is ready to fly and leave the nest.

Flightless bird A bird that is naturally unable to fly, such as a penguin or an ostrich.

Flock A group of animals.

Habitat The natural home of an animal or plant.

Mate An animal's partner for breeding.

Migration A seasonal journey that an animal makes, usually in order to feed or breed.

Murmuration A gathering of a large group of birds, usually starlings, that fly and change direction together.

Nectar A sweet liquid produced by flowers that animals like to eat.

Nocturnal Active at night.

Plankton Tiny living things, including plants and animals, that float in fresh or seawater.

Predator An animal that hunts and eats other animals.

Prey An animal that is hunted and eaten by other animals.

Rain forest A thick forest found in warm, wet areas of the world.

Roost To settle down to rest or sleep.

Talons The claws of a bird of prey.

Tropical Characteristic of an area of the world that is warm or hot all year round.